Re·ju·ve·na·tion

ENERGY • VITALITY • WELL-BEING

A 3-Week Alkalizing, Joint Health & Detoxification Program

Dr. Donald L. Hayes, D.C.

President, Wellness Watchers International, Inc.

Re·ju·ve·na·tion

Wellness Watchers International, Inc.

Wellness Watchers International, Inc.
(866-410-1818)

First Edition, 2007

The information in this book is not intended to be used as medical advice. The intent is solely informational and educational. Please consult a medical or health provider prior to starting this or any exercise, diet or dietary supplement program.

Library of Congress Cataloging-in-Publication Data

Hayes, Donald L.
Rejuvenation
A 3-Week Alkalizing Joint Health & Detoxification Program
Donald L. Hayes, DC – 1st ed.

1. Joint Health   2. Detoxification   3. Weight Management

I. Donald L. Hayes, DC   II. Title

Printed and bound in the United States of America. Ed. by John M. Jurcheck

ISBN: 1-4243-1855-6

Table of Contents

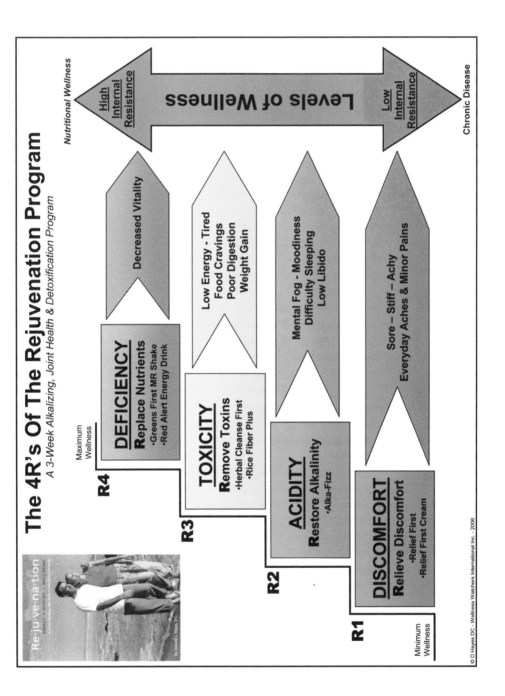

The 4R's Of The Rejuvenation Program
A 3-Week Alkalizing, Joint Health & Detoxification Program

Levels of Wellness

Nutritional Wellness

High Internal Resistance

Low Internal Resistance

Chronic Disease

Maximum Wellness

Minimum Wellness

R4

DEFICIENCY
Replace Nutrients
•Greens First MR Shake
•Red Alert Energy Drink

Decreased Vitality

R3

TOXICITY
Remove Toxins
•Herbal Cleanse First
•Rice Fiber Plus

Low Energy - Tired
Food Cravings
Poor Digestion
Weight Gain

R2

ACIDITY
Restore Alkalinity
•Alka-Fizz

Mental Fog - Moodiness
Difficulty Sleeping
Low Libido

R1

DISCOMFORT
Relieve Discomfort
•Relief First
•Relief First Cream

Sore – Stiff – Achy
Everyday Aches & Minor Pains

© D Hayes DC - Wellness Watchers International Inc. - 2006

Introduction

Welcome To The Rejuvenation Program

What Is The Rejuvenation Program?

Re·ju·ve·na·tion is defined in the Merriam-Webster Dictionary as being from the Latin root, juvenis, and means "to make young or youthful again; give new vigor to; to restore to an original or new state!

We live in a world overburdened with synthetic chemicals and toxins that find a way into our body and joints. Our bodies are inundated with toxins and chemicals from multiple sources, including from the polluted air we breathe, the treated water we drink, the chemicals we apply to our skin, and of course from the nutrient depleted, non-organic, processed foods we eat.

The Rejuvenation Program is a simple 3-week program to detoxify, deacidify, and cleanse the body and joints of toxins and chemicals, while restoring alkalinity and replacing vital nutrients.*

The lungs, liver, kidneys, colon, skin and lymphatic system are the major players responsible for the neutralization of stored acids and the elimination of toxins and chemicals from the body. *This is where the Rejuvenation Program can help!*

As soon as you turn the page, the process can begin…

CHAPTER ONE

Because Of Our Toxic Environment
Extra Rejuvenation Is Needed

The **Rejuvenation Program** uses nutrient-dense whole food supplements, clean food, and pure water to provide the body with the "tools" it must have to rejuvenate, "make youthful, and give new vigor," and to cleanse itself naturally.*

Vital Nutrients In & Unwanted Toxins Out
The **Rejuvenation Program** may help you improve your energy and vitality, while helping to increase your overall well-being through the elimination of toxins and replacement of vital nutrients.

Toxins In Our World
Chemicals and toxins in everyday products are ruining our health. Billions of pounds of toxic chemicals are released into our atmosphere every year, including million of pounds of known carcinogens. Every day, our bodies suffer a constant battle with toxins. In addition, our own bodies produce waste by-products as part of the normal digestive and metabolic system that must also be dealt with and eliminated. If toxins and chemicals from both external and internal sources are not neutralized and eliminated, poor health and disease can result.

Toxins In Our Body

Toxicity is an unavoidable consequence of living in a world full of synthetic chemicals. A healthy body is an efficient eliminator of toxins. Our colon and kidneys work daily to eliminate what they can. Breathing eliminates toxic carbon dioxide from our lungs. Our liver filters our blood supply of toxins. Our lymph system removes toxins and excess fluids from the body, as do our sweat glands. Any restriction or malfunction of these systems can cause toxins to build up and acids to accumulate, and illness or disease may result.

We can tolerate a certain level of toxins and acidity, but each person's level of tolerance is unique to them. Your level of tolerance will depend on many things, including your exposure levels, your lifestyle, your diet, drug use, medical treatments, personal environment, and the strength of your immune system.

Are You Toxic & Acidic?

Reflecting on the following questions will give you an opportunity to gauge your own possible level of toxicity and or acidity.

- Do you use sugar substitutes or eat foods that contain sugar substitutes or sweeteners?
- Do you eat non-organic fruits, vegetables, grains, meats (all types), or dairy foods (all types)?
- Do you ever drink tap water at home or at restaurants?
- Do you live or work in an area that has painted walls or ceilings?
- Do you use cosmetics, hair colorings, aftershaves, deodorants, lotions or perfumes?
- Do you eat microwave foods that come packaged with plastic wrap?
- Do you eat fat-free foods or snacks made with fat substitutes?
- Do you breathe polluted air?
- Do you drink non-organic coffee?
- Do you drink soda?
- Do you grill foods?
- Do you drink alcohol?

Your total number of YES answers determines your relative toxicity and acidity level. This of course is not a scientific test or health evaluation; it simply suggests the possible extent to which you are acidic and or carry a toxic load of chemicals.

As you have no doubt noticed, you're toxic and acidic even if you answered only a couple of questions in the affirmative. Toxicity and acidity varies only by degree. If you answered YES to a number of questions, it's likely that your diet and lifestyle are contributing significantly to your level of acidity and load of toxic chemicals.

In addition to your diet, you are also no doubt exposed to other outside toxins. This continuous onslaught of acids and chemicals from poor diet and outside sources may build up a level of toxins that creates such a burden on the body that it may have you feeling less than vital and experiencing:

- Fatigue or exhaustion
- Sore, stiff and achy joints
- Poor sleep habits
- Poor digestion
- Weight gain
- Mental fog and moodiness
- Cravings for sugar or processed food
- Low libido

CHAPTER TWO

What Does pH & Acid/Alkaline Balance Have To Do With Health?

The pH measures the balance of acidity and alkalinity in the body. When testing the acidity of the body, the arterial blood for example, you are testing pH. When testing pH, the result is a number from 0 to 14. Neutral is 7, with lower numbers representing an acidic condition and higher numbers representing an alkaline condition.

Our bodies are alkaline by design. All of the cells that make up the body are slightly alkaline and must stay that way to remain healthy and alive. The optimum range of body pH is from 7.2 to 7.6—slightly alkaline, with the normal level for arterial blood being 7.4.

Why Do We Become Acidic & Toxic and Need To Alkalize Our Body?

The pH measures the condition of critical bodily fluids. These fluids make up the internal environment that is critical to our health. Simply stated, an acid system is conducive to sickness, while alkalinity is required for normal healthy cellular functioning.

Every living cell within our body creates acidic waste products! Nutrients from the food we eat are delivered to each cell and burn with oxygen to provide energy for us to live. The by-products of this metabolic process are waste products. Virtually all waste products are acidic and therefore must be discharged from our body, typically disposed of through urination, perspiration and exhaling carbon dioxide.

One of the possible causes of the aging process and a host of potential chronic conditions is the accumulation of acidic wastes in the body due to years of having low-grade acidosis and a corresponding lowered blood pH.

It is now believed by many authorities that most adult degenerative conditions develop due to the degrading of the function and resistance of the body by chronic acidosis. Acidosis is thought to precede and cause disease. The well body succumbs to physical disorders when its own acid debris accumulates to the point where resistance is broken down and the body becomes susceptible to cold, fatigue, nerve exhaustion, and eventually degenerative disease.

Why Is It So Difficult To Keep Our Body Alkaline?
Our bodies are in a constant state of metabolizing. The problem is that the process of metabolism creates acid, which is needed for energy and other biochemical processes. Normal healthy metabolism creates acid wastes such as cholesterol, uric acid and acetic acid. Even with the best diet, these acid wastes are unavoidable, but they must be neutralized and eliminated from the body or harsh consequences will result.

To further compound the problem, our food, water and air are loaded with acid-forming substances like chlorine and an increasing assortment of chemicals. Soft drinks, especially colas (pH 2.5), are extremely acid forming and are the mainstay of our children's diets. Poor choices of foods, acidic ingredients and low mineral content all contribute to a condition of acid overload. Maintaining a proper, slightly alkaline pH is considered the most important aspect of a healthy body and a long, disease-free life. An imbalance of alkalinity creates a condition favorable to the growth of bacteria, viruses, yeast and other harmful organisms.

Accumulations of acid wastes are also closely linked with degenerative conditions, lack of vitality and aging in general. Even when there are no toxic substances in our food, there are waste products that must either be eliminated or stored. Toxins change into poison and must be detoxified or they will eventually destroy the system.

Our Bodies' Detoxification Defense System

The human body has an incredible ability to maintain life; however the compensations our bodies make come at a considerable price. As the toxins and acidic wastes accumulate over a period of years, we may experience no obvious ill effects but eventually the bill comes due and we pay the price.

Having toxic and acidic buildup is like driving your car with the oil light on. The car will continue to run without any apparent problem but, eventually, it will simply stop. To maintain life, our blood and cells must be defended against all of this acidity. Should we become

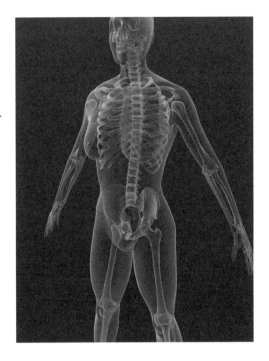

too acidic, we would die. Fortunately we have what amounts to an alkaline mineral bank in the bicarbonate reserves in our body. To buffer the acid overload the body makes withdrawals from this bank account. While this is effective in the short term, in the long run our bicarbonate reserves become depleted and our bones become more brittle with age, which can result in bone mass loss.

Another way the body alkalizes the blood and raises the pH is by solidifying acids in the blood and depositing them as solid wastes in the tissues of the body. This enables our blood to remain in an acceptable alkaline pH range, but as these harmful by-products accumulate, overall pH lowers (i.e. becomes more acidic), oxygen levels fall, and the seeds of a variety of degenerative conditions are sowed. This process of gradually depleting minerals from the bones and building up acidic deposits in body tissues is a slow one. For many years we have no symptoms, no warning of the storm that is building. Eventually we begin to experience aches, soreness and stiffness in the joints of our body, declining energy levels, and other subtle signs that we associate with getting older. These are not an inevitable part of getting older—they are warning signs. Many adult chronic conditions are directly associated with an acid pH and a low-grade acidosis. The **Rejuvenation Program** helps to deacidify your system and restore vital alkalinity.

CHAPTER THREE

Detoxification May Help Make You Thin!

One of the most important "side benefits" of the **Rejuvenation Program** is healthy weight loss. Both of the programs recommended are so incredibly low in calories and rich in nutrients and fiber that the more you eat of them the more weight you will lose! Of course, results do vary and have much to do with how closely you follow the program and how much exercise you add as well.*

A common solid acid waste that the body makes out of the excess acid in the bloodstream is fatty acid, which is stored in the body's "fat cells". Weight gain is a very common result of toxicity and over acidity.

Toxicity, acid buildup and weight gain can occur from eating a diet of nutrient deficient, high-calorie foods, often called "empty-calorie" or "junk" foods. "Empty calorie" means the food is deficient in nutrients and fiber. More people than ever before are eating these rich, high-calorie foods while remaining inactive, which is a dangerous combination. The number one health problem in the United States is weight gain. The National Institute of Health estimates that being overweight is associated with a twofold increase in mortality, costing society more than $100 billion per year.

This is especially discouraging for dieters because, after spending so much money attempting to lose weight, 95 percent of them gain all the weight back and then add on even more pounds within three years. This incredibly high failure rate holds true for the vast majority of weight-loss schemes, programs and diets.

The most beneficial and healthy weight management program takes time. Therefore, the program must be one that is easy on the system and easy to implement. It must focus on fat-loss not weight-loss, making sure not to lose valuable muscle mass. This may only be achieved if the weight management program is focused on maintaining an alkaline environment and providing the vital and dense nutrients the body needs. A successful and healthy weight management program must incorporate a way to detoxify, deacidify, and cleanse the body and joints, while at the same time restoring the critically low alkaline reserves and depleted nutrients.

The **Rejuvenation Program** uses nutrient-dense whole food supplements, clean food, and pure water to provide the body with what it needs to help rejuvenate itself and rid the "fat cells" of unwanted and unnecessary excess body fat.*

CHAPTER FOUR

Benefits Of The Rejuvenation Program

It's hard to believe, but almost all people with everyday aches and minor joint pain improve by following one of the two options in The **Rejuvenation Program**. Without a doubt, that probably has to do with the programs' ability to detoxify, deacidify, and cleanse the body and joints of toxins and chemicals, while restoring alkalinity and replacing vital depleted nutrients. The body has the chance to heal itself when the obstacles to healing, or stressors, are removed and the nutrient "tools" are provided.* Sometimes, however, people on the program will experience a "Healing Crisis."

What's A Healing Crisis?

Imagine if you drink fifteen cups of coffee a day and one day decide to stop all together. There's no question about it—you would feel it. You might immediately get headaches, start to feel weak and possibly even get the shakes. This would resolve itself slowly over four to six days and then you would feel fine. The same is true if you crave and eat nutrient-depleted processed foods.

A heavy coffee drinker or processed food addict feels the worst when they first wake up in the morning, after a forced 8-hour fast, or if they go too long between cups or a meal. Why? The body goes through withdrawals when it's not busy digesting a heavily processed meal or a recent cup of coffee. A nutrient-depleted processed meal or a cup of coffee will stop the ill feelings for a while but the cycle of feeling ill will start all over again the minute the caffeine level drops or the glucose level in the blood starts to go down.

Delaying a meal or a cup of coffee brings about symptoms most people call "hunger." These symptoms include abdominal cramps, weakness and feeling ill, the same as a person feels with drug withdrawal. This is not true hunger. Our dietary habits, especially eating nutrient-depleted, non-organic, processed foods three times a day, and drinking excessive caffeine-ridden drinks, are so stressful on the body's detoxification system, the liver and kidneys, that we start to get withdrawals or symptoms the minute we aren't processing these items. True hunger is not that uncomfortable.

You could feel better by drinking a cup of coffee every three hours, spaced out, to keep your caffeine blood levels constant, but I hope you understand that tempo-rarily feeling better does not mean getting well. Putting toxic food and drinks in your body can only compromise your health and lead to further dependence and discomfort. In other words, when you detoxify you may temporarily feel worse, not better. That will mean you're probably going through a Healing Crisis, and after the withdrawal symptoms have passed, you'll truly become well!

Re·ju·ve·na·tion

What To Do If You Experience A Healing Crisis

When you begin your Rejuvenation Program, you may notice a variety of changes, as noted above. Questions on how you feel or what you are experiencing should be directed to your health provide.

Remember, you should check with your own health provider before starting this or any diet or fitness program, and continue to direct questions to them if the need arises.

Which Rejuvenation Program Is Best For You?

Everyone is an individual and because of that, each of you are at a different level of fitness, have different food preferences and different goals. Because of that individuality, we provide you with two different Rejuvenation Program options to choose from. You and your health provider should decide together which option is best for you. Whichever one you choose, what is most important is that you complete the entire 3-Week program.

CHAPTER FIVE

The Rejuvenation Program Products

After selecting either the Non-Vegetarian or Vegetarian option in the **Rejuvenation Program**, your health provider will recommend that you use the following products:

- Relief First Kit
- Alka-Fizz
- Herbal Cleanse First
- Rice Fiber Plus
- Greens First Meal Replacement Shake
- Red Alert Energy Drink

Relief First Kit is a muscle and joint health package that works first topically with Relief First Cream, a soothing topical product that helps provide relief of muscle tenderness, joint stiffness and discomfort, and then systemically with Relief First capsules, a patented all-natural COX-2 inhibitor that supports joint health and helps to relieve everyday aches and minor pains that may contribute to overall joint health.*

Alka-Fizz is a potassium bicarbonate supplement that is designed to help neutralize acid and bring about an acid/alkaline balance to help stabilize blood pH. Alka-Fizz is not a medicine to cure any disease. There is no approved thera-peutic claim, but it will add bicarbonates [HCO3] to the bloodstream. Bicarbon-ates in the bloodstream are one of the primary substances for life and basic ele-ments of nutrition that keep your blood alkaline and available to neutralize acids. Consuming Alka-Fizz is like constantly renewing the battery of life! There's no more effective way to add bicarbonates and maintain proper potassium-sodium balance and acid/alkaline balance as consuming Alka-Fizz.*

Herbal Cleanse First is a 7-day, round-the-clock, cleansing support pro-gram. There are two separate formulas; one to be taken during the day with meals and the other to be taken before retiring for the night. **Daytime Detox:** The daytime formula is a blend of herbs including dandelion root, milk thistle and uva ursi, to help detoxify your system of impurities. **Nighttime Cleanse:** The nighttime formula is a fiber blend designed to help move impurities out of your system. When both formulas work together, they give the support your body may need to cleanse, detoxify and rejuvenate.*

Rice Fiber Plus caplets contain nutritional fiber, significant quantities of gamma oryzanol and several other phytonutrients, which can be part of an effective cleanse or detoxification, and part of a nutritionally balanced diet focused on healthy weight management. The product may help to support normal blood sugar levels because it may help to assist the body in reducing the level of insulin required to process food. The stabilized rice bran contained in the product may help to promote normal cholesterol levels. The majority of dietary fiber products on the market are psyllium based. Most of these products produce carbon dioxide and methane in the intestinal tract, which can produce bloating, gas and discomfort! **Rice Fiber Plus** caplets are made with stabilized rice bran, which is a "friendly nutritional fiber," promoting regularity and alleviating occasional constipation, while helping your body digest food more quickly and easily!*

Greens First Meal Replacement Shake is a delicious, complete meal replacement that helps to alkalize your body's pH for vibrant health! It's an easy and delicious way to improve energy, restore vitality and maximize your health! It can be used as a healthy "fast food" meal or snack that's delicious, low calorie and packed with nutrients!*

Each **Greens First Meal Replacement Kit** contains a can of **Greens First**, **Dream Protein**, and a bottle of **Complete Essentials** Ultra Pure Omega 3-6-9. Simply mix a scoop of **Greens First** and **Dream Protein** in 6 to 8 ounces of water or your favorite beverage and take 1 **Complete Essentials** Ultra Pure Omega 3-6-9 softgel!*

Red Alert Energy Drink is the perfect energy boosting companion to **Greens First**. If you're a busy professional or "on the go" parent, **Red Alert** provides a delicious and convenient way to enjoy many of the phytonutrients and antioxidant benefits of a fruit and vegetable rich diet...everyday! **Red Alert** has more fruits than vegetables and it is the perfect afternoon energy drink to keep you going strong without stimulants or artificial ingredients that can harm your health.*

CHAPTER SIX

What Do The 4R's Stand For in The Rejuvenation Program?

R1: DISCOMFORT

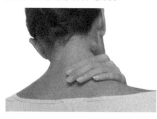

The first **"R"** in the **Rejuvenation Program** stands for **Relieving Discomfort** of everyday sore, stiff and achy joints. The product recommended is **The Relief First Kit**, which consists of both the **Relief First** capsules and the **Relief First Cream.*** (See the Discomfort Special Report for more specific details. You can obtain an instant copy of the report through your health provider's FirstShake.com website or contact them directly.)

R2: ACIDITY

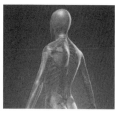

The second **"R"** in the **Rejuvenation Program** stands for **Restoring Alkalinity.** The product recommended is Alka-Fizz, which may help to neutralize the load of built-up acids in the body.* (See the Acidity Special Report for more specific details. You can obtain an instant copy of the report through your health provider's FirstShake.com website or contact them directly.)

R3: TOXICITY

The third **"R"** in the **Rejuvenation Program** stands for Removing Toxins. The product recommended is **Herbal Cleanse First**. (See the Toxicity Special Report for more specific details. You can obtain an instant copy of the report through your health provider's FirstShake.com website or contact them directly.)

R4: DEFICIENCY

The fourth **"R"** in the **Rejuvenation Program** stands for **Replacing Nutrients**. The products recommended are the **Greens First Meal Replacement Shake** and the **Red Alert Energy Drink**.* (See the Deficiency Special Report for more specific details. You can obtain an instant copy of the report through your health provider's FirstShake.com website or contact them directly.)

Basic Rejuvenation Guidelines

Combining regular exercise, proper eating habits and "whole food" dietary supplements is the best way to detoxify, deacidify, and cleanse the body and joints of toxins and chemicals, while restoring alkalinity and replacing vital depleted nutrients.*

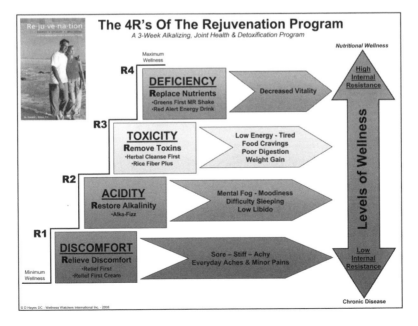

Here are the basic **Rejuvenation Program** guidelines to help:

- **R**elieve sore, stiff and achy joints.
- **R**estore alkaline reserves and neutralize accumulated acids.
- **R**emove as many toxins as possible from the body.
- **R**eplace vital nutrients in the body on a daily basis.

Follow the recommended **Rejuvenation Program**.

By following these simple guidelines, you may be able to detoxify, deacidify, and cleanse the body and joints of toxins and chemicals, restore alkaline reserves, replace vital depleted nutrients, improve your energy, reduce many chronic symptoms, and lose weight.*

Please be patient!

Toxin buildup, acid accumulation and weight gain did not happen overnight, so expect to take at least a reasonable period of time to detoxify. Follow the **Rejuvenation Program** suggested by your health provider and you may be able to take back control of your energy, health and life!

CHAPTER SEVEN

Basics For The Rejuvenation Program

What have you learned so far? A large amount of nutrient-depleted processed foods in your diet is bad for your health and correlates with acid production, toxicity, a decrease in alkaline reserves, a possible increase in body fat, and could become the basis for a chronic disease.

Two Program Options:
- Non-Vegetarian Program
- Vegetarian Program

Both Program Options Are 3-Week Plans
Get ready for the most exciting 3 weeks of your life. If you follow one of the two options programs as outlined for the next 3 weeks, your body will undergo a remarkable transformation and you will be witness to its miraculous self-healing ability. With no compromise for the next three weeks, you will unleash a biochemical and physiological makeover that may change you forever. You will be thrilled with how easily your weight drops and the subtle changes you experience in your physical and mental well-being. Perhaps even more meaningfully than the weight loss, you will feel better than you have in years.

Most get so excited with the results during the 3-week "trial," that they are motivated to keep going. Results encourage change, and results motivate. The stricter you are, the more quickly your taste will change. The 3-week plan gives your body time to adjust to this new way of eating. At the beginning the weight comes off quickly, but as you approach your target weight, your weight loss will slow down.

Your taste buds will change. They will actually become more sensitive to the subtle flavors in natural foods, and 3 weeks is a sufficient period of time for any symptoms arising from the new diet to subside.

CHAPTER EIGHT

The Rejuvenation Program

OPTION ONE - Non-Vegetarian Program

The Non-Vegetarian Program is the first option in the Rejuvenation Program. It consists of eating whole foods that contain abundant vitamins, minerals, phytochemicals and antioxidants that may help to support all major detoxification organs and systems in the body during the 3-week Rejuvenation Program.

Diet Selection - Non-Vegetarian Program

For the duration of the 3-week program eat only the items listed below, in addition to the recommended supplements. Use organic fruits and vegetables, free-range, grass-fed meats, free-range eggs, and wild fish if possible.

Select Vegetables & Fruits From The List In Chapter Nine

- Unlimited salads daily.
- Unlimited raw vegetables daily.
- Unlimited steamed or cooked green vegetables daily.
- Unlimited beans or legumes daily.
- Unlimited fresh fruit daily.
- One serving of starchy vegetables or grains once daily.

- One to two grams of omega-3 fat once daily.
- 3-4 ounces of unseasoned lean meat, fish or poultry twice daily.
- 1-2 egg whites per day.

Supplementation - Non-Vegetarian Program

The **Relief First Kit: Relief First Capsules & Relief First Cream** are recommended throughout the 3-Week **Rejuvenation Program** as needed and directed by your health provider. **Herbal Cleanse First** is recommended for week one only, and **Alka-Fizz, Rice Fiber Plus, Greens First Meal Replacement Shake** and **Red Alert Energy Drink** are recommended throughout the entire program.

Week One
- 2 **Relief First** capsules 2 times a day, or as directed by health provider
- **Relief First Cream** as needed, or as directed by health provider
- 3 Daytime **Herbal Cleanse First** tablets, 3 times daily
- 3 Nighttime **Herbal Cleanse First** tablets in evening, prior to bed
- 1 **Alka-Fizz packet**, 1 time a day
- 3 **Rice Fiber Plus** caplets, 2 times daily
- 1-2 **Greens First Meal Replacement Shakes** per day. First within 30 minutes of rising.
- 1-2 **Red Alert Energy Drinks** per day. 10AM & 2PM

Weeks Two & Three
- 2 **Relief First** capsules 2 times a day, or as directed by health provider
- **Relief First Cream** as needed or directed by health provider
- 1 **Alka-Fizz** packet, 1 time a day
- 3 **Rice Fiber Plus** caplets, 2 times daily
- 1-2 **Greens First Meal Replacement Shakes** per day. First within 30 minutes of rising.
- 1-2 **Red Alert Energy Drinks** per day. 10AM & 2PM

NOTE: Alka-Fizz should be taken with water. All other supplements should be taken with a Greens First Meal Replacement Shake, a Red Alert Energy Drink or water, but not with meals. Supplements can be taken one hour before or two hours after a meal.

Exercise - Non-Vegetarian Program

It's recommended that you walk four to five times per week for 30 to 60 minutes. This is important to get your detoxification and lymphatic systems functioning properly. Strenuous exercise should be avoided while on the 3-week program. Consult your health provider if you are currently on an exercise program that you would like to continue throughout the entire **Rejuvenation Program**. If you are not exercising, make sure you check with your health provider before you start. Refer to Chapter 3 "Exercise" in the *7 Habits of Healthy Living* book for the best exercise plan for you. This book is available online at your health provider's FirstShake.com website or through their office directly.

OPTION TWO – The Vegetarian Program

The **Vegetarian Program** is the second option in the **Rejuvenation Program**. It consists of eating only fruits and vegetables and excluding all animal products, dairy, cheese, and oils. This program may also help to support all major detoxification organs and systems in the body during the 3-Week **Rejuvenation Program**.

Nutrient-dense natural plant foods, though usually carbohydrate rich, also contain protein and fats. On average, 25 percent of the calories in vegetables are from protein. Romaine lettuce, for example, is rich in both protein and essential fatty acids, giving us those healthy fats our bodies require. There's no longer any question about the importance of fruits and vegetables in our diet. The greater the quantity and assortment of fruits and vegetables consumed, the lower the incidence of chronic disease. This means that your risks decrease with an increased intake of fruits and vegetables and the earlier in life you start eating large amounts of these foods, the more protection you get.

Diet Selection - Vegetarian Program

For the duration of the 3-week program, eat only the items listed below in addition to the recommended supplements. Use organic fruits and vegetables if possible.

Select Vegetables & Fruits From The List In Chapter Nine

- Unlimited salads daily.
- Unlimited raw vegetables daily.
- Unlimited steamed or cooked green vegetables daily.
- Unlimited beans or legumes daily.
- Unlimited fresh fruit daily.
- One serving of starchy vegetables or grains once daily.
- One to two grams of omega-3 fat once daily.

Supplementation - Vegetarian Program

The **Relief First Kit: Relief First Capsules & Relief First Cream** are recommended throughout the 3-Week **Rejuvenation Program** as needed and directed by your health provider. **Herbal Cleanse First** is recommended for week one only, and **Alka-Fizz, Rice Fiber Plus, Greens First Meal Replacement Shake** and **Red Alert Energy Drink** are recommended throughout the entire program.

Week One
- 2 **Relief First** capsules 2 times a day, or as directed by health provider
- **Relief First Cream** as needed, or as directed by health provider
- 3 Daytime **Herbal Cleanse First** tablets, 3 times daily
- 3 Nighttime **Herbal Cleanse First** tablets in evening, prior to bed
- 1 **Alka-Fizz packet**, 1 time a day
- 3 **Rice Fiber Plus** caplets, 2 times daily
- 1-2 **Greens First Meal Replacement Shakes** per day. First within 30 minutes of rising.
- 1-2 **Red Alert Energy Drinks** per day. 10AM & 2PM

Weeks Two & Three
- 2 **Relief First** capsules 2 times a day, or as directed by health provider
- **Relief First Cream** as needed or directed by health provider
- 1 **Alka-Fizz** packet, 1 time a day
- 3 **Rice Fiber Plus** caplets, 2 times daily
- 1-2 **Greens First Meal Replacement Shakes** per day. First within 30 minutes of rising.
- 1-2 **Red Alert Energy Drinks** per day. 10AM & 2PM

NOTE: Alka-Fizz should be taken with water. All other supplements should be taken with a Greens First Meal Replacement Shake, a Red Alert Energy Drink or water, but not with meals. Supplements can be taken one hour before or two hours after a meal.

Exercise - Vegetarian Program

It's recommended that you walk four to five times per week for 30 to 60 minutes. This is important to get your detoxification and lymphatic systems functioning properly. Strenuous exercise should be avoided while on the 3-week program. Consult your health provider if you are currently on an exercise program that you would like to continue throughout the entire **Rejuvenation Program**. If you are not exercising, make sure you check with your health provider before you start. Refer to Chapter 3 "Exercise" in the *7 Habits of Healthy Living* book for the best exercise plan for you. This book is available online at your health provider's FirstShake.com website or through their office directly.

CHAPTER NINE

Raw Vegetables & Salads

These foods are to be eaten in unlimited quantities, regardless of which program you choose, but always think big! Since they have a negative calorie effect, the more you eat, the more you detox and the more you lose. Raw foods also have a faster transit time through the digestive tract and result in a lower glucose response and encourage more weight loss than cooked ones. Plus, in terms of detoxification, these foods are fantastic! During the 3-week program use only fat-free dressings or lemon juice.

The object is to eat as much salad and as many raw vegetables as possible. Eating an entire head of romaine or the equivalent amount of a green lettuce every day would not be too much.

Include raw vegetables such as:
- Snow peas
- Sweet red peppers
- Raw peas
- Tomatoes
- Cucumbers
- Sprouts.

An entire pound of lettuce and raw vegetables is less than 100 calories of food!

Steamed or Cooked Green Vegetables

Eat as much as you can from this group as well, again with the idea that the more you eat the more you will detox and the more weight you will lose. One of your keys to success with this program is to eat a decent amount of food, so when you eat these green vegetables, try to eat a much larger portion than you might have in the past. Completely rethink what your idea of a portion is – make it huge!

Go for variety in your cooked vegetables by using:

• String beans	• Broccoli	• Artichokes
• Asparagus	• Zucchini	• Kale
• Collards	• Cabbage	• Brussels sprouts
• Bok choy	• Okra	• Swiss chard
• Turnip greens	• Beet greens	• Water chestnuts
• Spinach	• Escarole	• Dandelion greens
• Cauliflower	• Eggplant	• Peppers

Beans & Legumes

Legumes are among the world's most perfect foods. They stabilize blood sugar, blunt your desire for sweets, and prevent mid-afternoon cravings. Even a small portion can help you feel full, but in the 3-week plan you are encouraged to eat at least one full cup daily. You can eat unlimited quantities of them.

Among Your Choices For Beans and Legumes Are:

• Chickpeas (Garbanzo Beans)		• Black-eyed peas
• Black beans	• Cowpeas	• Red kidney beans
• Lima beans	• Pinto beans	• Lentils
• Green peas	• Soy beans	• Cannelloni beans
• White beans		

Fresh Fruit

Eat at least four fresh fruits per day, but no fruit juice. Cut up apples and oranges are excellent added to a salad and will help you feel full. On the 3-week plan, no fruit juice is permitted except small quantities for salad dressings and cooking. Juicing fruits allows us to quickly consume three times the calories, without the fiber to regulate absorption. The nutrient-per-calorie ratio is much higher for the whole food. Frozen fruit is permissible, but avoid canned fruit because it is not as nutritious. Dried fruits are off-limits as well during the 3-week plan.

Eat A Variety Of Fruit Such As:
- Apples
- Apricots
- Bananas
- Blackberries
- Blueberries
- Dates
- Figs
- Grapefruits
- Grapes
- Kiwis
- Kumquats
- Mangoes
- Melons
- Nectarines
- Oranges
- Papayas
- Peaches
- Pears
- Persimmons
- Pineapples
- Plums
- Raspberries
- Strawberries
- Tangerines

Starchy Vegetables & Grains

These two food categories are grouped together because either can be the culprit for those who have difficulty losing weight. While wholesome, these cooked high-starch vegetables are more calorie dense than the non-starchy vegetables listed above, so they should be limited to one serving daily. Diabetics or those that want to lose weight more rapidly and those who have difficulty losing weight may want to restrict these foods altogether, at least until they have arrived at their target weight. Eating lots of greens makes it difficult to overeat high-starch vegetables. You just won't have room for that much.

Examples Of Starchy Vegetables Include:
- Carrots
- Corn
- Sweet potatoes
- Acorn squash
- White potatoes
- Butternut squash
- Winter squash
- Chestnuts
- Parsnips
- Rutabagas
- Turnips
- Yams

Grains Include:
- Whole wheat
- Barley
- Buckwheat
- Millet
- Oats
- Quinoa
- Brown rice
- Wild rice

Nuts & Seeds

Nuts and seeds contain 150-200 calories per ounce. Eating a small amount of one ounce or less each day adds valuable nutrients and healthy unprocessed fats. Nuts and seeds are ideal in salad dressings. Always eat nuts and seeds raw because the roasting process alters their beneficial fats. Commercially packaged nuts and seeds are often cooked in hydrogenated oils, adding trans fats and sodium to your diet, so these are absolutely off the list.

Among The Raw Nuts And Seeds You Can Add To Your Diet Are:
- Almonds
- Cashews
- Sunflower seeds
- Pecans
- Filberts
- Sesame seeds
- Walnuts
- Pumpkin seeds
- Flaxseed

Fats & Oils

Your body must burn 23% of the calories consumed from carbohydrates to make the conversion from glucose to body fat, but it converts food fat into body fat quickly and easily. One hundred calories of ingested food fat can be converted to ninety-seven calories of body fat, burning only three calories. So the fat you eat is easily and rapidly stored by the body.

Converting food fat into body fat is easy; the process doesn't even change the molecules. Researchers can actually take fat biopsies of your hips or waist and tell you where it came from—pig fat, dairy fat, chicken fat or olive oil; the fat is still the same as it was on your plate, but now it's under your skin. Fat is also an appetite stimulant—the more you eat, the more you want! With that said, it's true that most of us eat too much fat, but research also reveals that too little of the right kind of fat can be a problem too. Most of us are not only consuming too much fat but more importantly consuming the wrong fats.

The standard American diet is full of vegetable oils and animal products that are very high in omega-6 fat and very low in omega-3 fat. The consumption of too much omega-6 fat leads to high levels of arachidonic acid that can promote inflammation. When we don't have enough omega-3 fat we don't produce enough DHA, which has anti-inflammatory effects.

Both meat-based diets and vegetarian diets can be deficient in these healthy fats if they do not contain sufficient green leaves, beans, nuts, seeds or fish. So eat less of the fatty foods you usually consume and eat more walnuts, flaxseed, soybeans and leafy green vegetables.

Vegetarians and non-vegetarians should make an effort to consume one to two grams of omega-3 fat daily. A tablespoon of ground flaxseed contains approximately 1.7 grams of omega-3 fat while 4 tablespoons of walnuts contain 2 grams.

CHAPTER TEN

Is This A Low Calorie Program?

Yes, actually it is. Excess calories don't just make you overweight, they shorten your life. You may already know that almost all diets are ineffective. The conventional solution to being overweight, low-calorie dieting, doesn't work. The reason is due to a simple concept overlooked by most people, and that is that being overweight is not caused by *how many* calories they eat, but *what* calories they eat.

The idea that people get fat because they eat a lot of food is a myth. Eating large amounts of the right food is your key to success with this program. What makes many people overweight is not that they eat so much more but that they get a higher percentage of their calories from fat, refined carbohydrates and mostly nutrient-deficient foods. This low-nutrient diet establishes a favorable cellular environment for acid buildup, toxins and everyday aches and minor pains to occur in the joints of the body.

The **Rejuvenation Program** enables people to feel satiated with 1,000 to 2,000 calories per day, whereas before it may have taken 1,600 to 3,000 or more. The simple trick is to receive lots of nutrients from each calorie you consume. Of course, those that are very active will get more calories, more protein and other nutrients they need by consuming more food, not by following a different diet.

Some people can lose weight by switching their calories to a healthier plant-based diet, while maintaining the same caloric consumption. The Chinese consume more calories than do Americans, yet are about 25% thinner than Americans. This is because the modern American diet receives about 37% of its calories from fat, with lots of sugar and refined carbohydrates. The combination of high fat and high sugar is a metabolic disaster that causes weight gain, independent of the number of calories.

Other people are not able to lose weight as easily. They need the metabolic benefit of the natural plant foods, along with the satisfaction that comes from the greater bulk of "unlimited" foods and the consequent nutrient fulfillment. These people need even fewer calories. The good news is that on this program they can be satisfied with fewer calories permanently.

The 80/20 Rule Makes It Work In The Real World

Remember—your purpose in going on the **Rejuvenation Program** is to detoxify, deacidify, and cleanse your body and joints of toxins and chemicals, while restoring alkalinity and replacing vital depleted nutrients.

At the end of the 3-week program, you can continue to benefit from the program by making sure your ongoing diet is made up of at least 80% unrefined plant foods. You should treat processed foods and animal foods as side dishes, contributing no more than 20% or less of your total calorie intake. This approach will significantly reduce the amount of animal foods, dairy and processed foods in your diet. If you desire these foods, use them occasionally or in very small amounts to flavor a vegetable dish.

If after the 3-Week Vegetarian Program (**Rejuvenation Program**, Option Two) you want to introduce animal products back into your diet, then add a little white-meat chicken or turkey once a week, and beef even less frequently. This will essentially limit your total animal-product consumption (beef, turkey, fish) to 12 ounces or less per week.

Likewise, if after the 3-week you choose to reintroduce dairy back into your diet, use fat-free dairy only, such as skim milk or nonfat yogurt, and limit it to 12 ounces per week.

Using the 80/20 rule means that you are allowed to eat almost any kind of food, even a small cookie or candy bar, as long as all your other calories that day are from nutrient-dense vegetation.

What Do I Do If I "Fall Off" My Program?

Get back on! Since the goal is to eat at least 80% or your diet from nutrient-dense plant foods, if you fall off the plan in one area, make up for it in another. If you eat all the recommended amounts of green vegetables, beans and fruit, you will have consumed fewer than 1000 calories of nutrient-dense food, with as much as 40 grams of fiber. By consuming so many crucial nutrients and fiber, your body's desire to overeat is curtailed.

With either program option, you will consume more than ten times the phytochemicals and ten times the fiber that most Americans consume. Keep in mind that it's the full spectrum of nutrients in natural whole foods that offers the greatest protection for maximum health and rejuvenation.

Is Exercise Essential For Success On The Program?

Exercise is important and will facilitate your success to detoxify, deacidify, and cleanse your body and joints of toxins and make you healthier. As mentioned previously, it is recommended that you walk four to five times per week for 30-60 minutes. This is important to get your detoxification and lymphatic systems functioning properly. Strenuous exercise should be avoided while on the 3-week program. Consult with your health provider if you are currently on an exercise program that you would like to continue throughout the **Rejuvenation Program**. If you are not exercising, make sure you check with your health provider before you start. Refer to Chapter 3 "Exercise" in the 7 *Habits of Healthy Living* book for the best exercise plan for you. This book is available online at your health provider's FirstShake.com website or through their office directly.

CHAPTER TEN

Rejuvenation Program Meal Plans

When it comes to nutrition, there are certain standards that are important to note when you are on the 3-Week **Rejuvenation Program**. It is important to choose non-genetically modified (Non-GMO) organic fruits, vegetables and grains. Try to choose free-range, hormone and antibiotic-free meat, diary, eggs and poultry. Many regular supermarkets are increasing their selection of these healthful alternatives! The pesticides and exogenous hormones that you may be exposed to when you consume "conventional" or "non-organic" foods add to the toxicity that we are trying to eliminate during this period.

Cooking Tips

• We suggest limiting your intake of salt and processed sugar during this program. Also use cooking methods such as broiling, poaching, sautéing, steaming and stir-frying. These methods result in food that is higher in nutrients and fiber and lower in fat, cholesterol, sugar, and salt.

• When you are stir-frying veggies, try to use organic chicken broth or vegetable broth with your favorite herbs, spices and garlic to add flavor to your recipe instead of using olive oil.

~ 7-Day Meal Plans ~

NON-VEGETARIAN PROGRAM

These Non-Vegetarian Meal Plans are similar to the Vegetarian Meal Plans, but, of course, they will include a small amount of animal foods to flavor the soups and casseroles, as well as being part of the main course for dinner meals. This meal plan does have a few more recipes that may include some vegetables with a slightly higher starch content. We are also including one teaspoon of healthy oil as an option.

On this Meal Plan, no cheese is recommended for the 3-week period because of the high saturated fat content. No more than 12 ounces of animal products per week is also recommended.

Most of these recipe suggestions can be adapted for those wanting to stay on the Vegetarian Meal Plan. Simply leave out the animal products and the oil. When sautéing vegetables, cook in a small amount vegetable broth with your favorite spices instead of oil. Add a bit more broth until the vegetables become tender.

If weight loss is also a goal, we recommend that you may want to eat smaller portions of the high-starch vegetables such as white potatoes, sweet potatoes or yams, and high-starch fruits such as bananas, figs, prunes and dried fruit. Also, do not use oil. As mentioned in the previous paragraph, use a small amount of vegetable broth with your favorite spices, instead of oil, to cook onions and vegetables until tender.

Selections with this image ⌒ after the words indicate that there is a recipe in the **Rejuvenation Recipes** section.

NON-VEGETARIAN PROGRAM

Day One

Breakfast

- Greens First Meal Replacement Shake [Within the first 30 minutes upon arising]. Add one scoop of Greens First and one scoop of Dream Protein to 8 ounces of pure water in a shaker cup. [Hint: Put water in first!] Shake well.
- Along with your shake, take 1 Complete Essentials Omega softgel capsule.
- 1-2 Seasonal fresh fruits

Lunch

- Half a section of whole-wheat pita bread, toasted on both sides. Add thin slices of turkey breast, tomatoes, thin slices of red and green peppers and romaine lettuce.
- Add a fat-free dressing of your choice.
- Seasonal fresh fruit

Dinner

- Fresh mixed green salad with cucumbers, carrots, red, yellow and green peppers (or a variety of your favorite veggies)
- Add 1tsp. of fat-free dressing
- Dijon Chicken Breast Supreme 📖
- 1 or 2 Seasonal fresh fruits

Day Two

Breakfast

- Greens First Meal Replacement Shake [Within the first 30 minutes upon arising]. Add one scoop of Greens First and one scoop of Dream Protein to 8 ounces of pure water in a shaker cup. [Hint: Put water in first!] Shake well.
- Along with your shake, take 1 Complete Essentials Omega softgel capsule.
- 1-2 Seasonal fresh fruits

Lunch

- Spinach Salad with Red Onions, Pear Slices and Garbanzo Beans
- Fresh oranges and lemons squeezed over as dressing
    - Optional: Fat-free or low-fat dressing of your choice
- 2-3 low-fat, high-fiber rice crackers
- 1-2 Seasonal fresh fruits

Dinner
- Mixed Herb Lettuce and Yellow & Red Small Tomatoes, Cucumbers and Celery
- Fat-free or low-fat dressing of your choice
- Broiled Halibut with Sun-Dried Tomatoes ⌂
- Blackberry Peach Swirl ⌂

Day Three

Breakfast
- **Greens First Meal Replacement Shake** [Within the first 30 minutes upon arising]. Add one scoop of Greens First and one scoop of Dream Protein to 8 ounces of pure water in a shaker cup. [Hint: Put water in first!] Shake well.
- Along with your shake, take 1 Complete Essentials Omega softgel capsule.
- 1-2 Seasonal fresh fruits

Lunch
- Assortment of favorite raw veggies with creamy fat-free dressing dip
- Organic Canned Chicken Vegetable Soup
- Fruit Bowl with pureed strawberries on top, sprinkled with 1 ounce crushed walnuts.
- Dust with cinnamon.

Dinner
- Salad with Romaine Lettuce, Assorted Veggies and Orange Slices. Sprinkle with mixture of orange juice and lemon for dressing.
- Savory Beef Burritos ⌂
- Corn on the Cob with garlic lemon pepper.
- Frozen orange juice pops.

Day Four

Breakfast
- **Greens First Meal Replacement Shake** [Within the first 30 minutes upon arising]. Add one scoop of Greens First and one scoop of Dream Protein to 8 ounces of pure water in a shaker cup. [Hint: Put water in first!] Shake well.
- Along with your shake, take 1 Complete Essentials Omega softgel capsule.
- 1-2 Seasonal fresh fruits

Lunch
- Spinach Salad with chopped Red Onions, Orange Sections and 1 ounce slivered Almonds
- Fat-free dressing of your choice
- Artichoke hearts, dipped in fat-free or low-fat dressing
- Fresh strawberries and blueberries
- 1 ounce of nuts

Dinner
- Romaine Lettuce Spears in Orange & Lime Juice
- Basil Turkey Breast over Noodles
- Fresh Steamed Broccoli with Lemon & Garlic Pepper
- Baked Apples with Raisins and Cinnamon

Day Five

Breakfast
- **Greens First Meal Replacement Shake** [Within the first 30 minutes upon arising]. Add one scoop of Greens First and one scoop of Dream Protein to 8 ounces of pure water in a shaker cup. [Hint: Put water in first!] Shake well.
- Along with your shake, take 1 Complete Essentials Omega softgel capsule.
- 1-2 Seasonal fresh fruits

Lunch
- Lentil & Bean Soup
- Whole Wheat Pita Bread and zesty Black Bean Hummus
- Fruit Bowl with pureed Raspberry and 1 ounce chopped walnuts sprinkled over top

Dinner
- Mixed Green Salad with favorite cut of Veggies, topped with Fat-Free Dressing
- Bean Pasta Stew
- Steamed frozen organic veggies sprinkled with fresh dill and lemon garlic pepper
- Fresh Fruit Bowl with sliced Kiwis

Day Six

Breakfast

- Greens First Meal Replacement Shake [Within the first 30 minutes upon arising]. Add one scoop of Greens First and one scoop of Dream Protein to 8 ounces of pure water in a shaker cup. [Hint: Put water in first!] Shake well.
- Along with your shake, take 1 Complete Essentials Omega softgel capsule.
- 1-2 Seasonal fresh fruits

Lunch

- Curried Turkey Macaroni Salad ⌂ (Hint: Make the day before)
- Sliced Tomatoes drizzled with zesty non-fat Italian Dressing and lemon pepper
- Celery Stalks with Spicy Black Bean Dip
- 1-2 fresh fruits

Dinner

- Poached Salmon with Dilled Cucumbers ⌂
- Steamed fresh green beans with sautéed onions and mushrooms
- Boiled red potatoes with lemon garlic pepper
- Raspberry Poached Pears with Cinnamon ⌂

Day Seven

Breakfast

- Greens First Meal Replacement Shake [Within the first 30 minutes upon arising]. Add one scoop of Greens First and one scoop of Dream Protein to 8 ounces of pure water in a shaker cup. [Hint: Put water in first!] Shake well.
- Along with your shake, take 1 Complete Essentials Omega softgel capsule.
- 1-2 Seasonal fresh fruits

Lunch

- Assortment of Raw Veggies dipped in Creamy Non-Fat Dressing
- Italian Chicken Salad ⌂
- Green Apple slices in Lime Juice

Dinner

- Boston Lettuce with chopped Red Onion, Sliced Pear, White Mushrooms with Orange Vinegar.
- Angel Hair Pasta with Shrimp 🥘
- Steamed vegetables
- Fresh pineapple slices

NON-VEGETARIAN RECIPES

• Angel Hair Pasta with Shrimp   Serves 4

1 (16-ounce) package capellini (angel hair) pasta
1/4 cup olive oil
2 tablespoons fresh parsley, chopped
2 cloves garlic, finely chopped
1 small red chili, seeded and finely chopped
1/3 cup dry white wine ~ or ~ 1/3 cup vegetable broth
1/2 teaspoon freshly grated nutmeg
3/4 pound uncooked, peeled, de-veined small shrimp, thawed if frozen

1. Cook and drain pasta as directed on package.
2. While pasta is cooking, heat oil in Dutch oven or 12-inch skillet over medium-high heat. Cook parsley, garlic and chili in oil for 1 minute, stirring occasionally. Stir in wine, nutmeg and shrimp; reduce heat. Cover and simmer for about 5 minutes or until shrimp are pink and firm.
3. Combine pasta and shrimp mixture in Dutch oven. Cook over medium heat for 2 minutes, stirring occasionally.

• Basil Turkey Breast over Noodles   Serves 4

1-2 teaspoons olive oil ~ or ~ vegetable broth
1 medium onion, finely chopped (1/2 cup)
1 clove garlic, finely chopped
3 medium tomatoes, seeded and chopped (2 1/4 cups)
2 cups cubed turkey breast
1/4 cup chopped fresh basil
1/2 teaspoon sea salt
2 cups uncooked cholesterol-free noodles [whole-wheat noodles, if possible] (4 ounces)

Heat oil in 10-inch nonstick skillet over medium-high heat. Cook onion and garlic in oil or vegetable broth, stirring occasionally, until onion is tender. Stir in remaining ingredients, except noodles; reduce heat to medium. Cover and cook for about 5 minutes, stirring frequently, until mixture is hot and tomatoes are soft. Meanwhile, cook and drain noodles as directed on package. Serve turkey breast mixture over hot noodles.

• Bean Pasta Stew   Serves 4

2 (15-ounce) cans pinto beans, rinsed and drained

~ or ~

2 (15-ounce) cans navy beans, rinsed and drained
1 (14 1/2-ounce) can Italian-style stewed tomatoes, un-drained
1 (14 1/2-ounce) can ready-to-serve chicken broth
1 (10-ounce) package frozen cut green beans, thawed
2 medium stalks celery, sliced (1 cup)
1 1/2 teaspoons Italian seasoning
1/2 cup uncooked small pasta shells (2 ounces)

Bring all ingredients, except pasta, to a boil in a 3-quart saucepan; reduce heat to low. Stir in pasta. Cover and simmer for about 15 minutes, stirring occasionally, until pasta is tender.

• Black Bean Hummus Spread or Dip   Serves 4

1 (15 ounce) can black beans, rinsed and drained
15 ounces garbanzo beans (chick peas), rinsed and drained
1/2 cup water ~ or ~1/2 cup bean liquid
3 tablespoons lemon juice
2 tablespoons olive oil
1 teaspoon sesame oil
1/4 teaspoon ground cumin
Salt and pepper to taste
2 cloves garlic, finely chopped
2 tablespoons chopped fresh parsley
Pita bread or raw vegetables, if desired

Place all ingredients except parsley and pita bread in blender. Cover and blend on medium speed until smooth. Place in serving bowl. Sprinkle with parsley. Cover and refrigerate for about 2 hours or until chilled. Serve with whole-wheat pita bread.

- **Blackberry Peach Swirl**   Serves 4
2 cups Oregon blackberries, fresh or frozen
1 12-ounce can peach nectar
2 teaspoons lemon juice
3 tablespoons sugar (or equivalent amount of stevia)
16 ounces crushed ice (approximate)
Sparkling mineral water (optional)

Crush/purée berries and strain through a fine sieve to yield approximately 1 cup of purée. (If berries are frozen, partially thaw before crushing.) Combine purée with remaining ingredients, stir and pour into chilled glasses. Sparkling mineral water makes a nice addition and may be added to glasses if desired.

- **Broiled Halibut with Sun-Dried Tomatoes**   Serves 2
2- 6 oz Halibut Filets
Sun-dried tomato halves (packed in water)
1/4 cup fat-free salad dressing
2 tablespoons chopped fresh parsley
1/8 teaspoon pepper

Set oven control to broil. Grease rack of broiler pan. Place fish on rack in broiler pan. Broil with tops 4 inches from heat for 8 minutes. Soak tomato halves in 1 cup very hot water for about 5 minutes or until softened; drain and finely chop. Mix with remaining ingredients, then spread on fish. Broil 1 to 2 minutes longer or until topping is light brown and fish flakes easily with fork.

- **Curried Turkey Macaroni Salad** (Hint: Make the day before)   Serves 4
1 1/2 cups uncooked elbow macaroni (approximately 6 ounces)
1 (10 ounce) package frozen green peas
3/4 cup non-fat creamy salad dressing
2 teaspoons curry powder
2 cups cooked organic turkey breast, cut-up
1/2 cup cheddar-like soy cheese (2 ounces), shredded
4 medium green onions (1/4 cup), sliced
1 medium stalk celery (1/2 cup), sliced
Lettuce leaves, if desired

1. Cook and drain macaroni as directed on package. Rinse with cold water; drain. Rinse frozen peas with cold water to separate; drain.

2. Mix non-fat creamy salad dressing and curry powder in large bowl. Stir in macaroni, peas and remaining ingredients, except lettuce. Cover and refrigerate 2 to 4 hours to blend flavors. Serve on lettuce.

• **Dijon Chicken Breast Supreme**   Serves 4-6

3 pounds skinless boneless chicken breast halves (about 6 small)
1/4 cup Dijon mustard
1 teaspoon olive oil (optional)
2 tablespoons dry white wine
Freshly ground pepper
2 tablespoons mustard seeds
Chopped parsley, if desired

Heat oven to 400°. Remove excess fat from chicken. Place chicken, meaty sides up, in rectangular pan, 13 × 9 × 2 inches, sprayed with nonstick cooking spray. Mix mustard, oil, and wine; brush over chicken. Sprinkle with pepper and mustard seeds. Bake uncovered until chicken is done, for about 30 minutes. Sprinkle with chopped parsley.

• **Italian Chicken Salad**   Serves 4

3/4 cup uncooked fusilli or rotini pasta
1/2 cup zesty non-fat Italian dressing
1 medium yellow or green bell pepper (1 cup), chopped
1 medium carrot (2/3 cup), shredded
4 boneless, skinless chicken breast halves (about 1 pound)
6 cups Italian blend or mixed-greens salad, bite-size pieces

1. Cook and drain pasta as directed on package. Toss pasta and 1/3 cup of the dressing. Stir in bell pepper and carrot.

2. Cover and grill chicken 4 to 6 inches from medium coals for 15 to 20 minutes, brushing with remaining dressing and turning occasionally, until juice of chicken is no longer pink when centers of thickest pieces are cut. Cut chicken diagonally into 1-inch strips.

3. Divide salad greens among 4 serving plates. Top with pasta mixture and chicken. Sprinkle with pepper if desired.

• Poached Salmon with Dilled Cucumbers   Serves 4
4 salmon steaks (1 1/2 pounds)
1 tablespoon chopped fresh dill weed ~ or ~ 1/2 teaspoon dried dill weed
1/4 teaspoon sea salt
1/4 cup water
1 tablespoon lemon juice
Dilled Cucumbers (recipe follows)

Place fish in 10-inch nonstick skillet. Sprinkle with dill weed and sea salt. Pour water and lemon juice into skillet. Heat to boiling; reduce heat. Cover and cook for 15 to 20 minutes or until fish flakes easily with fork. Meanwhile, prepare Dilled Cucumbers. Serve over fish.

DILLED CUCUMBERS
1 medium cucumber, peeled
1 tablespoon chopped fresh dill weed ~ or ~ 1 teaspoon dried dill weed
1 tablespoon white vinegar
1/4 teaspoon salt
Dash of Lemon Pepper

Cut cucumber in half lengthwise; seed and cut into thin slices. Mix cucumber and remaining ingredients in 1 1/2-quart saucepan. Cook over high heat for 1 to 2 minutes, stirring frequently, until cucumber is crisp-tender.

• Raspberry Poached Pears   Serves 4
1/2 cup seedless raspberry spreadable fruit (similar to jam but 100% fruit)
1 cup apple juice
2 teaspoons grated lemon peel
2 tablespoons lemon juice
3 firm Bosc pears, peeled and cut into fourths
Dash of cinnamon

Mix all ingredients except pears in 10-inch skillet. Add pears. Heat to boiling; reduce heat to medium-low. Simmer uncovered for 30 minutes, spooning juice mixture over pears and turning every 10 minutes, until pears are tender. Serve warm or chilled.

• **Savory Beef Burritos**   Serves 4-6

2 cups shredded cooked beef (use hormone-free beef, if possible)
1 cup canned fat-free refried beans (from 16 ounce can)
        ~ or ~ 1 can of spicy black beans
8 flour tortillas (8 to 10 inches in diameter), warmed
2 cups shredded romaine lettuce
2 medium tomatoes, chopped (1 1/2 cups)
1 cup shredded reduced-fat cheddar cheese (4 ounces)
Salsa, if desired

Heat beef in 1-quart saucepan over medium heat, stirring occasionally, until warm.
Heat beans in 1-quart saucepan over medium heat, stirring occasionally, until
warm. Fold up bottom third of each tortilla; roll up to form a cone shape, with
folded end at bottom. Spoon beans, beef, lettuce, tomatoes and cheese into cone.
Serve with salsa.

~ 7-Day Meal Plans ~

VEGETARIAN PROGRAM

Day One

Breakfast

> • Greens First Meal Replacement Shake [Within the first 30 minutes
> upon arising]. Add one scoop of Greens First and one scoop of Dream
> Protein to 8 ounces of pure water in a shaker cup. [Hint: Put water
> in first!] Shake well.
> • Along with your shake, take 1 Complete Essentials Omega softgel capsule.
> • 1-2 Seasonal fresh fruits

Lunch

> • Assortment of Raw Veggies dipped in Creamy Non-Fat Dressing
> • Rice & Bean Roll Ups 🗀
> • Fresh (or frozen) Blackberry and Raspberry Mixture topped with dash of
> cinnamon

Dinner

- Mixed Green Salad sprinkled with Orange Juice and Shredded Pear
- Roasted Vegetable Lasagna 🍞
- Corn on the Cob with Garlic Pepper
- Fresh Strawberries

Day Two

Breakfast

- **Greens First Meal Replacement Shake** [Within the first 30 minutes upon arising]. Add one scoop of Greens First and one scoop of Dream Protein to 8 ounces of pure water in a shaker cup. [Hint: Put water in first!] Shake well.
- Along with your shake, take 1 Complete Essentials Omega softgel capsule.
- 1-2 Seasonal fresh fruits

Lunch

- Celery Stalks with Spicy Black Bean Dip
- Artichoke Hearts dipped in Creamy Non-Fat Dressing
- Frozen Mixed Blueberries, Blackberries & Raspberries

Dinner

- Mixed Green Salad with Thin Slivers of Green Apple and 1 oz. Chopped Walnuts
- Basil-Tarragon Vegetable Bake 🍞
- Baked Potato with Spicy Salsa
- Kiwis

Day Three

Breakfast

- **Greens First Meal Replacement Shake** [Within the first 30 minutes upon arising]. Add one scoop of Greens First and one scoop of Dream Protein to 8 ounces of pure water in a shaker cup. [Hint: Put water in first!] Shake well.
- Along with your shake, take 1 Complete Essentials Omega softgel capsule.
- 1-2 Seasonal fresh fruits

Lunch
- Salad Stuffed Whole Wheat Pita with Hummus
- Celery & Carrot Stalks dipped in Creamy Fat-Free Dressing
- 1 – 2 pieces of seasonal fresh fruit

Dinner
- Romaine Lettuce soaked in Orange Juice, sprinkled with Dried Cranberries
- Three Bean Chili 🖃
- Corn on the Cob with Favorite Seasonings
- Frozen Blueberries

Day Four

Breakfast
- **Greens First Meal Replacement Shake** [Within the first 30 minutes upon arising]. Add one scoop of Greens First and one scoop of Dream Protein to 8 ounces of pure water in a shaker cup. [Hint: Put water in first!] Shake well.
- Along with your shake, take 1 Complete Essentials Omega softgel capsule.
- 1-2 Seasonal fresh fruits

Lunch
- Sautéed Mushrooms on Fresh Mixed Salad Greens 🖃
- Raw Veggies with Black Bean Dip
- Applesauce topped with Thinly Sliced Bananas, 1 ounce of Crushed Walnuts and Dusted with Cinnamon

Dinner
- Mixed Baby Greens with Non-Fat or Low-Fat Peppercorn Dressing
- Tomatoes Stuffed With Rice & Vegetables 🖃
- Steamed Green Beans with Red & Yellow Pepper Slices & Slivered Almonds topped with Garlic Powder
- Fresh Strawberries and Blueberries

Day Five

Breakfast
- **Greens First Meal Replacement Shake** [Within the first 30 minutes upon arising]. Add one scoop of Greens First and one scoop of Dream Protein to 8 ounces of pure water in a shaker cup. [Hint: Put water in first!] Shake well.
- Along with your shake, take 1 Complete Essentials Omega softgel capsule.
- 1-2 Seasonal fresh fruits

Lunch
- Tacos (Tempeh or Tofu) ⌂
- Green Apple Slices in Lime Juice
- 1 oz sunflower seeds

Dinner
- Mixed Baby Greens with Sliced Pears
- Non-Fat or Low-Fat Dressing of Choice
- Honey-Herbed Vegetables over Brown Rice ⌂
- Baked Apple with Crushed Walnuts and Cinnamon

Day Six

Breakfast
- *Greens* First Meal Replacement Shake [Within the first 30 minutes upon arising] Add one scoop of Greens First and one scoop of Dream Protein to 8 ounces of pure water in a shaker cup. [Hint: Put water in first!] Shake well.
- Along with your shake, take 1 Complete Essentials Omega softgel capsule.
- 1-2 Seasonal fresh fruits

Lunch
- Romaine Lettuce Salad with Cucumbers, Red, Yellow & Green Peppers and small Sugar Plum Tomatoes.
- Fat-Free Italian Dressing
- Vegan Split Pea Soup ⌂
- 1 or 2 pieces of seasonal fresh fruit

Dinner
- Mixed Green Herb Salad with thin slivers of Organic Green Apple
- Roasted Mushrooms with Winter Vegetables ⌂
- Steamed Broccoli with Lemon
- Fresh fruit

Day Seven

Breakfast

- Greens First Meal Replacement Shake [Within the first 30 minutes upon arising]. Add one scoop of Greens First and one scoop of Dream Protein to 8 ounces of pure water in a shaker cup. [Hint: Put water in first!] Shake well.
- Along with your shake, take 1 Complete Essentials Omega softgel capsule.
- 1-2 Seasonal fresh fruits

Lunch

- Raisin Coleslaw ⌐
- Veggie Burger with lettuce and tomatoes on a Whole Wheat Bun
- Fresh berries topped with soy yogurt and a dash of cinnamon

Dinner

- Mixed Baby Greens Salad with Tomatoes, Cucumbers, Zucchini and Red Onions.
- Fat-Free Dressing
- Veggie Stir-Fry ⌐
- Mixed Blackberries & Raspberries in Melons (Cantaloupe or Honeydew) with a squeeze of lime

VEGETARIAN RECIPES

• Basil-Tarragon Vegetable Bake   Serves 4

1 pound broccoli (1 small bunch), cut into flowerets and 1-inch pieces
1 small head cauliflower (about 1 1/4 pounds), cut into flowerets
5 carrots (about 1 pound), cut diagonally into 1/4 inch slices
1/4 - 1/3 cup vegetable broth
Dash of sea-salt and garlic lemon pepper
1 tablespoon chopped fresh basil leaves ~ or 1 teaspoon dried basil leaves
1 tablespoon chopped fresh tarragon leaves ~ or ~ 1 teaspoon dried tarragon
    leaves
2 cloves garlic, finely chopped
2 small onions, thinly sliced and separated into rings
        Optional: Top with salsa

Heat oven to 400°. Arrange broccoli along one long side of ungreased rectangular baking dish, 13 × 9 × 2 inches. Arrange cauliflower along other side of dish. Arrange carrots down center between broccoli and cauliflower. Drizzle with vegetable broth. Sprinkle with salt, pepper, basil, tarragon and garlic. Arrange onions evenly over top.

Cover with aluminum foil and bake for about 30 minutes or until vegetables are crisp-tender

• Honey-Herbed Vegetables over Brown Rice   Serves 4

1/4 cup honey
2 tablespoons onion, minced
1/4 to 1/2 cup of vegetable broth
1/2 teaspoon thyme, crushed
6 cups vegetables of your choice: peas, zucchini, spinach, broccoli, green beans
Cooked brown rice
Salt and pepper, to taste

Combine all ingredients in a small saucepan and bring to a boil; cook for 2 minutes. Toss with vegetables of choice such as: peas, zucchini, spinach, broccoli, green beans, etc. Serve over cooked brown rice as an entrée or alone as a side dish.

• Raisin Coleslaw   Serves 4

1/2 cup raisins
1/2 cup apple juice
1/2 baked potato with skin removed
1 teaspoon mustard
1 tablespoon lemon juice
4 cups cabbage, shredded
2 cups carrots, shredded
1 cup beets, shredded (optional)
2 cups apples, peeled and shredded
1/4 cup scallion, finely chopped

Blend or Vita-Mix raisins, apple juice, potato, mustard, and lemon juice. Then mix all ingredients together.

• Rice & Bean Roll Ups   Serves 3

1 1/2 cups thick-and-chunky salsa
1 cup cooked brown rice
2 medium Roma (plum) tomatoes, chopped
1 small bell pepper, cut into 1/2-inch pieces (1/2 cup)
1 (15-ounce) can black beans with cumin, undrained
1 (8-ounce) can whole kernel corn, drained
6 jalapeño-flavored or whole wheat flour tortillas (8 to 10 inches in diameter)

Heat oven to 350°. Spread 1/2 cup of the salsa in ungreased rectangular baking dish, 13 × 9 × 2 inches.

Mix rice, tomatoes, bell pepper, beans and corn. Spread 3/4 cup rice mixture on each tortilla; roll up. Place seam sides down on salsa in baking dish. Spoon the remaining 1 cup salsa over tortillas.

Cover and bake 30 to 35 minutes or until heated through.

• Roasted Mushrooms with Winter Vegetables   Serves 4

12 ounces fresh white mushrooms
4 ounces shiitake mushrooms
5 medium-size sweet potatoes (about 2 pounds)
2 medium onions (about 8 ounces)
12 large cloves garlic
1/4 to 1/2 cup vegetable broth divided
1 tablespoon chopped fresh rosemary ~ or 1 1/2 teaspoons crushed dried rosemary
1 teaspoon sea salt
1/2 teaspoon ground black pepper

Preheat oven to 425° F. Trim white mushrooms. Remove and discard shiitake stems. Peel and cut sweet potatoes in half lengthwise, then into 1/2-inch slices. Cut onions into 1-inch wedges. Cut garlic cloves in halves. In a large bowl, combine broth, rosemary, salt and pepper. Add mushrooms, sweet potatoes, onions and garlic; toss to coat. In two shallow roasting pans, arrange vegetables in a single layer. Roast, stirring once, until tender, for about 25 minutes.
    (Mixture can be roasted in advance and reheated in a hot oven.)

• Roasted Vegetable Lasagna   Serves 4

1/4 to 1/2 cup vegetable broth
2 medium bell peppers, cut into 1-inch pieces
1 medium onion, cut into 8 wedges and separated into pieces
2 medium zucchini, sliced (4 cups)
8 ounces mushrooms, sliced (3 cups)
1/2 teaspoon salt
1/4 teaspoon pepper
Tomato Sauce (below) ~ or ~ 1 (32-ounce) jar spaghetti sauce
12 uncooked lasagna noodles

TOMATO SAUCE
1/4 to 1/2 cup vegetable broth
1 large onion, chopped (1 cup)
2 tablespoons finely chopped garlic
1 (28-ounce) can crushed tomatoes, undrained
3 tablespoons chopped fresh basil ~ or ~ 1 tablespoon dried basil leaves
3 tablespoons chopped fresh oregano ~ or ~ 1 tablespoon oregano leaves
1/2 teaspoon sea salt
1/2 teaspoon crushed red pepper

Heat oven to 450°. Cover jelly roll pan or pan, 15 1/2 × 10 1/2 × 1 inch, with aluminum foil. Place bell peppers, onion, zucchini and mushrooms in single layer in pan. Drizzle vegetables with vegetable broth; sprinkle with salt and pepper. Bake uncovered 20 to 25 minutes, turning vegetables once, until vegetables are tender.

While vegetables are roasting, prepare Tomato Sauce. Cook and drain noodles as directed on package. Rinse noodles with cold water; drain.

Reduce oven temperature to 400°. Spread 1/4 cup of the sauce in dish; top with 3 noodles. Layer with 3/4 cup sauce, 1 1/4 cups vegetables. Repeat layers 3 more times with remaining noodles, sauce, and vegetable mixture. Top with thinly sliced tomatoes and dust with garlic lemon pepper.

Bake uncovered for 20 to 25 minutes or until hot. Let stand for 10 minutes before cutting.

TOMATO SAUCE
Cook onion and garlic in vegetable broth in saucepan over medium heat for 2 minutes, stirring occasionally. Stir in remaining ingredients. Heat to boiling; reduce heat. Simmer uncovered for 15 to 20 minutes or until slightly thickened.

• Sautéed Mushrooms on Fresh Mixed Salad Greens   Serves 4

1 pound fresh white mushrooms
4 ounces fresh shiitake mushrooms
6 to 12 tablespoons of vegetable broth, divided
1/4 cup cider or white wine vinegar
2 teaspoons Dijon-style mustard
1/2 teaspoon sea salt
1/4 teaspoon ground black garlic pepper
6 cups (about 8 ounces) mixed salad greens including arugula, radicchio and endive

Trim and slice white mushrooms. Remove and discard shiitake stems; slice caps.
To prepare dressing: In a cup, combine 4-6 tablespoons of the broth, the vinegar,
mustard, sea salt and garlic pepper; set aside. Just before serving: In a large skillet,
over low heat, heat 1-3 tablespoon of the broth. Add half of the mushrooms; cook
and stir until golden, for about 5 minutes; remove to a bowl. Repeat with remaining broth and mushrooms; return cooked mushrooms to skillet; heat until hot. Stir
in reserved dressing. Spoon over salad greens.

• Tacos (Tempeh or Tofu)   Serves 3

1 pound tempeh, defrosted and cut into large chunks ~ or ~ 1 pound tofu,
crumbled
2-4 tablespoons vegetable broth
1 package taco seasoning
1/2 cup water
6 corn tortillas, warmed
1 can brown or black beans
Chopped tomatoes, lettuce & scallions for garnish
Salsa

In a large saucepan, place the tempeh chunks in the broth. Crumble the tempeh
chunks with the back of a fork, then cook the tempeh (or the tofu) over medium
heat for about 10 minutes. Add the taco seasoning and water to the saucepan;
cook until the sauce is thick and the tempeh or tofu is completely coated.

To serve, spread each tortilla with a generous layer of the refried beans. Add several
heaped spoonfuls of tempeh or tofu. Sprinkle with chopped tomatoes, lettuce, and
scallions. Top with salsa.

• Three Bean Chili   Serves 6

1 large onion, chopped (1 cup)
2 cloves garlic, crushed
1 (14 1/2 ounce) can ready-to-serve vegetable broth
2 large tomatoes, seeded and cubed (2 cups)
2 tablespoons chopped fresh cilantro
1 tablespoon chopped fresh oregano leaves ~ or ~ 1 teaspoon dried oregano leaves
2 teaspoons chili powder
1 teaspoon ground cumin
1 (15 ounce) can kidney beans, undrained
1 (15 ounce) can garbanzo beans, undrained
1 (15 ounce) can spicy chili beans, undrained

Cook onion and garlic in 1/4 cup of the broth in nonstick Dutch oven over medium heat for about 5 minutes, stirring occasionally, until onion is crisp-tender. Stir in remaining broth and remaining ingredients, except beans. Heat to boiling; reduce heat. Cover and simmer for 30 minutes, stirring occasionally. Stir in beans. Heat to boiling; reduce heat. Simmer uncovered for about 20 minutes, stirring occasionally, until desired consistency.

• Tomatoes Stuffed With Rice & Vegetables   Serves 6

6 large fresh tomatoes
2-4 tablespoons vegetable broth
1 1/2 cups sliced fresh white mushrooms
1 cup chopped onion
1 10-ounce package frozen chopped spinach, thawed and drained
2 teaspoons minced garlic
1 teaspoon dried basil leaves, crushed
1/2 teaspoon salt ~ or ~ 1 chicken bouillon cube, crushed
1/4 teaspoon ground black pepper
1/2 cup quick-cooking rice
         Salsa - optional

Preheat oven to 400°F. Use tomatoes held at room temperature until fully ripe. Cut a slice from the top of each tomato; remove pulp, leaving a 1/4-inch thick shell; set aside. Chop tomato pulp (makes about 3-1/2 cups). In a large skillet over medium heat, add 2 to 4 tablespoons of vegetable broth. Add mushrooms and onion; cook and stir until tender, for about 10 minutes. Add spinach, reserved chopped tomatoes, garlic, basil, salt and pepper. Cook over low heat, stirring occasionally, until flavors blend, for about 10 minutes. Stir in rice. Remove from heat; cover and let stand for 5 minutes. Place tomato shells in a 13 × 9 × 2-inch baking pan. Spoon hot mixture into shells, dividing evenly. Put ¼ teaspoon of Salsa on top. Bake until tomatoes are hot and filling is golden, for about 15 minutes.

• Vegan Split Pea Soup   Serves 4

2 quarts water
1 pound split peas
1 large onion, chopped
1 cup celery, chopped
1 cup potatoes, diced
1 carrot, shredded
1/8 teaspoon Worcestershire sauce
1 teaspoon garlic powder
1/2 teaspoon celery seed
2 teaspoons sea salt
1/2 teaspoon garlic pepper

In large soup kettle, cover peas with 2 quarts water. Simmer for 2 minutes. Remove from heat. Add remaining ingredients. Mix. Simmer on low heat (do not boil) for 3-4 hours. When peas are tender, run 1/3 to 1/2 of soup through blender. Mix blended and unblended soups together. Adjust seasonings to taste.

• Veggie Stir-Fry   Serves 4

3/4 cup apple juice
2 tablespoons cornstarch
3 tablespoons reduced-sodium soy sauce
2-4 tablespoons vegetable broth
6 cups cut-up vegetables (such as 1-inch pieces of asparagus, sliced zucchini, cauliflowerets or broccoli flowerets)
1 medium onion, cut lengthwise in half, then cut crosswise into thin slices
1 clove garlic, finely chopped
3 tablespoons apple juice
1 (15-ounce) can garbanzo beans (15 to 16 ounces), rinsed and drained
Mix 3/4 cup apple juice, the cornstarch and soy sauce; set aside.

Heat wok or 12-inch nonstick skillet over medium-high heat. Add vegetable broth and rotate wok to coat side. Add vegetables, onion and garlic; stir-fry 1 minute. Add 3 tablespoons apple juice. Cover and cook for about 3 minutes or until vegetables are tender.

Stir in beans and soy sauce mixture; reduce heat to medium. Cook for about 3 minutes, stirring frequently, until sauce thickens.

Take Time For Health...It's Worth It!

It may take a little time and effort to finish this **Rejuvenation Program**... but you'll be glad you did!

If you follow the **Rejuvenation Program** as outlined in this book and stick to the 3 weeks of healthier eating, you will realize how great it is to be able to increase your energy, improve vitality and gain that overall sense of well-being.

You may also benefit in other ways, such as better sleep, less body fat, more strength, healthier skin, nails and hair, reduced cravings for sweets and stimulants, and not to mention you may experience fewer everyday aches and minor pains!

This is the end of the book, but, hopefully, it is just the beginning of a healthier you.

Good Luck To You!

I hope you continue your quest for health and happiness long after you've closed the last page in this book...

The Re·ju·ve·na·tion Journal
A 3-Week Alkalizing Joint Health & Detoxification Program

Welcome to the Rejuvenation Journal

As you progress through your chosen program, you may experience many highs and lows as your internal system attempts to detoxify, deacidify, and cleanse the body and joints of toxins and chemicals and restore alkaline reserves and replace vital depleted nutrients.

The lungs, liver, kidneys, colon, skin and lymphatic system will be the major players responsible for the neutralization of stored acids and the elimination of toxins and chemicals from the body for the next 3 weeks.

During this joint health and detoxification program you should make note of what you eat and drink and how you feel. You can use this journal to help you record your entire rejuvenation journey.

You may bring this journal with you when you visit your health provider. It may help them determine how you are progressing on the program and enable them to answer any questions that you may have on symptoms or progress.

EXAMPLE OF HOW TO FILL OUT THE JOURNAL

Date / Day
Enter the date and day number for each of the 3 weeks on the program.

Food & Drink
Write down briefly what you eat and drink during the day.

Symptoms
Note any physical symptoms you are experiencing.

Energy Level
List your level of energy or fatigue.

Exercise
Jot down all forms of activity or exercise.

Other
List any other detoxification measures or activities that may be relevant
to this program.

Re·ju·ve·na·tion
ENERGY • VITALITY • WELL-BEING

A 3-Week Alkalizing, Joint Health
& Detoxification Program

Date:_____ Day _____   [Record Both Food & Drink]

Breakfast:_____
_____
_____
_____

Lunch: _____
_____
_____
_____

Dinner: _____
_____
_____
_____

Snacks:_____
_____
_____
_____

Symptoms:_____
_____
_____
_____

Energy Level: _____
_____

Exercise: _____
_____
_____
_____

Other:_____
_____
_____

Re·ju·ve·na·tion

ENERGY • VITALITY • WELL-BEING

A 3-Week Alkalizing, Joint Health
& Detoxification Program

Date:_____ Day _____   [Record Both Food & Drink]

Breakfast:_____
_____
_____
_____

Lunch: _____
_____
_____
_____

Dinner: _____
_____
_____
_____

Snacks:_____
_____
_____
_____

Symptoms:_____
_____
_____
_____

Energy Level: _____
_____

Exercise: _____
_____
_____

Other:_____
_____
_____

Re·ju·ve·na·tion
ENERGY • VITALITY • WELL-BEING

A 3-Week Alkalizing, Joint Health
& Detoxification Program

Date:_____ Day _____   [Record Both Food & Drink]

Breakfast:_____
_____
_____
_____

Lunch: _____
_____
_____
_____

Dinner: _____
_____
_____
_____

Snacks:_____
_____
_____
_____

Symptoms:_____
_____
_____
_____

Energy Level: _____
_____

Exercise: _____
_____
_____
_____

Other:_____
_____
_____

Re·ju·ve·na·tion
ENERGY • VITALITY • WELL-BEING

A 3-Week Alkalizing, Joint Health
& Detoxification Program

Date:_____ Day _____   [Record Both Food & Drink]

Breakfast:_____
_____
_____
_____

Lunch: _____
_____
_____
_____

Dinner: _____
_____
_____
_____

Snacks:_____
_____
_____
_____

Symptoms:_____
_____
_____
_____

Energy Level: _____
_____

Exercise: _____
_____
_____

Other:_____
_____
_____

Re·ju·ve·na·tion

ENERGY • VITALITY • WELL-BEING

A 3-Week Alkalizing, Joint Health
& Detoxification Program

Date:_____ Day _____   [Record Both Food & Drink]

Breakfast:_____
_____
_____
_____

Lunch: _____
_____
_____
_____

Dinner: _____
_____
_____
_____

Snacks:_____
_____
_____
_____

Symptoms:_____
_____
_____
_____

Energy Level: _____
_____

Exercise: _____
_____
_____
_____

Other:_____
_____
_____

Re·ju·ve·na·tion

ENERGY • VITALITY • WELL-BEING

A 3-Week Alkalizing, Joint Health
& Detoxification Program

Date:_____ Day _____   [Record Both Food & Drink]

Breakfast:_____
_____
_____
_____

Lunch: _____
_____
_____
_____

Dinner: _____
_____
_____
_____

Snacks:_____
_____
_____
_____

Symptoms:_____
_____
_____
_____

Energy Level: _____
_____

Exercise: _____
_____
_____
_____

Other:_____
_____
_____

Re·ju·ve·na·tion
ENERGY • VITALITY • WELL-BEING

A 3-Week Alkalizing, Joint Health
& Detoxification Program

Date:_____ Day _____   [Record Both Food & Drink]

Breakfast:_____
_____
_____
_____

Lunch: _____
_____
_____
_____

Dinner: _____
_____
_____
_____

Snacks:_____
_____
_____
_____

Symptoms:_____
_____
_____
_____

Energy Level: _____
_____

Exercise: _____
_____
_____
_____

Other:_____
_____
_____

Re·ju·ve·na·tion
ENERGY • VITALITY • WELL-BEING

A 3-Week Alkalizing, Joint Health
& Detoxification Program

Date:_____ Day _____   [Record Both Food & Drink]

Breakfast:_____
_____
_____
_____

Lunch: _____
_____
_____
_____

Dinner: _____
_____
_____
_____

Snacks:_____
_____
_____
_____

Symptoms:_____
_____
_____
_____

Energy Level: _____
_____

Exercise: _____
_____
_____

Other:_____
_____
_____

Re·ju·ve·na·tion
ENERGY • VITALITY • WELL-BEING

A 3-Week Alkalizing, Joint Health
& Detoxification Program

Date:_____ Day _____   [Record Both Food & Drink]

Breakfast:_____
_____
_____
_____

Lunch: _____
_____
_____
_____

Dinner: _____
_____
_____
_____

Snacks:_____
_____
_____
_____

Symptoms:_____
_____
_____
_____

Energy Level: _____
_____

Exercise: _____
_____
_____
_____

Other:_____
_____
_____

Re·ju·ve·na·tion
ENERGY • VITALITY • WELL-BEING

A 3-Week Alkalizing, Joint Health
& Detoxification Program

Date:_____ Day _____   [Record Both Food & Drink]

Breakfast:_____
_____
_____
_____

Lunch: _____
_____
_____
_____

Dinner: _____
_____
_____
_____

Snacks:_____
_____
_____
_____

Symptoms:_____
_____
_____
_____

Energy Level: _____
_____

Exercise: _____
_____
_____

Other:_____
_____
_____

Re·ju·ve·na·tion
ENERGY • VITALITY • WELL-BEING

A 3-Week Alkalizing, Joint Health
& Detoxification Program

Date:_____ Day _____   [Record Both Food & Drink]

Breakfast:_____
_____
_____
_____

Lunch: _____
_____
_____
_____

Dinner: _____
_____
_____
_____

Snacks:_____
_____
_____
_____

Symptoms:_____
_____
_____
_____

Energy Level: _____
_____

Exercise: _____
_____
_____
_____

Other:_____
_____
_____

Re·ju·ve·na·tion

ENERGY • VITALITY • WELL-BEING

A 3-Week Alkalizing, Joint Health
& Detoxification Program

Date:_____ Day _____   [Record Both Food & Drink]

Breakfast:_____
_____
_____
_____

Lunch: _____
_____
_____
_____

Dinner: _____
_____
_____
_____

Snacks:_____
_____
_____
_____

Symptoms:_____
_____
_____
_____

Energy Level: _____
_____

Exercise: _____
_____
_____
_____

Other:_____
_____
_____

Re·ju·ve·na·tion
ENERGY • VITALITY • WELL-BEING

A 3-Week Alkalizing, Joint Health
& Detoxification Program

Date:_____ Day _____   [Record Both Food & Drink]

Breakfast:_____
_____
_____
_____

Lunch: _____
_____
_____
_____

Dinner: _____
_____
_____
_____

Snacks:_____
_____
_____
_____

Symptoms:_____
_____
_____
_____

Energy Level: _____
_____

Exercise: _____
_____
_____
_____

Other:_____
_____
_____

Re·ju·ve·na·tion
ENERGY • VITALITY • WELL-BEING

A 3-Week Alkalizing, Joint Health
& Detoxification Program

Date:_____ Day _____   [Record Both Food & Drink]

Breakfast:_____
_____
_____
_____

Lunch: _____
_____
_____
_____

Dinner: _____
_____
_____
_____

Snacks:_____
_____
_____
_____

Symptoms:_____
_____
_____
_____

Energy Level: _____
_____

Exercise: _____
_____
_____
_____

Other:_____
_____
_____

Re·ju·ve·na·tion
ENERGY • VITALITY • WELL-BEING

A 3-Week Alkalizing, Joint Health
& Detoxification Program

Date:_____ Day _____   [Record Both Food & Drink]

Breakfast:_____

_____

_____

_____

Lunch: _____

_____

_____

_____

Dinner: _____

_____

_____

_____

Snacks:_____

_____

_____

_____

Symptoms:_____

_____

_____

_____

Energy Level: _____

_____

Exercise: _____

_____

_____

_____

Other:_____

_____

_____

Re·ju·ve·na·tion
ENERGY • VITALITY • WELL-BEING

A 3-Week Alkalizing, Joint Health
& Detoxification Program

Date:_____ Day _____   [Record Both Food & Drink]

Breakfast:_____

_____

_____

_____

Lunch: _____

_____

_____

_____

Dinner: _____

_____

_____

_____

Snacks:_____

_____

_____

_____

Symptoms:_____

_____

_____

_____

Energy Level: _____

_____

Exercise: _____

_____

_____

_____

Other:_____

_____

_____

Re·ju·ve·na·tion
ENERGY • VITALITY • WELL-BEING

A 3-Week Alkalizing, Joint Health
& Detoxification Program

Date:_____ Day _____   [Record Both Food & Drink]

Breakfast:_____
_____
_____
_____

Lunch: _____
_____
_____
_____

Dinner: _____
_____
_____
_____

Snacks:_____
_____
_____
_____

Symptoms:_____
_____
_____
_____

Energy Level: _____
_____

Exercise: _____
_____
_____
_____

Other:_____
_____
_____

Re·ju·ve·na·tion
ENERGY • VITALITY • WELL-BEING

A 3-Week Alkalizing, Joint Health
& Detoxification Program

Date:_____ Day _____   [Record Both Food & Drink]

Breakfast:_____
_____
_____
_____

Lunch: _____
_____
_____
_____

Dinner: _____
_____
_____
_____

Snacks:_____
_____
_____
_____

Symptoms:_____
_____
_____
_____

Energy Level: _____
_____

Exercise: _____
_____
_____
_____

Other:_____
_____
_____

Re·ju·ve·na·tion
ENERGY • VITALITY • WELL-BEING

A 3-Week Alkalizing, Joint Health
& Detoxification Program

Date:_____ Day _____   [Record Both Food & Drink]

Breakfast:_____
_____
_____
_____

Lunch: _____
_____
_____
_____

Dinner: _____
_____
_____
_____

Snacks:_____
_____
_____
_____

Symptoms:_____
_____
_____
_____

Energy Level: _____
_____

Exercise: _____
_____
_____
_____

Other:_____
_____
_____

Re·ju·ve·na·tion
ENERGY • VITALITY • WELL-BEING

A 3-Week Alkalizing, Joint Health
& Detoxification Program

Date:_____ Day _____   [Record Both Food & Drink]

Breakfast:_____
_____
_____
_____

Lunch: _____
_____
_____
_____

Dinner: _____
_____
_____
_____

Snacks:_____
_____
_____
_____

Symptoms:_____
_____
_____
_____

Energy Level: _____
_____

Exercise: _____
_____
_____
_____

Other:_____
_____
_____

Re·ju·ve·na·tion
ENERGY • VITALITY • WELL-BEING

A 3-Week Alkalizing, Joint Health
& Detoxification Program

Date:_____ Day _____   [Record Both Food & Drink]

Breakfast:_____
_____
_____
_____

Lunch: _____
_____
_____
_____

Dinner: _____
_____
_____
_____

Snacks:_____
_____
_____
_____

Symptoms:_____
_____
_____
_____

Energy Level: _____
_____

Exercise: _____
_____
_____
_____

Other:_____
_____
_____

Disclaimer
The information contained in this book is for educational purposes only and is not meant to diagnose, treat or cure any disease and any statement made about any dietary nutritional supplement referenced has not been evaluated by the FDA. This information is not attempting to formally prescribe treatment. Any nutritional or fitness program that is started should first be discussed with your health care professional.

Neither the author nor publisher is engaged in rendering professional advice or services to the individual reader. The ideas, procedures, nutritional supplements and suggestions contained in this book and e-book are not intended as a substitute for consulting with your health care professional. All matters regarding your health require medical supervision. Neither the author nor the publisher shall be liable or responsible for any loss or damage allegedly arising from any information or suggestions in this book or e-book.

Reminder
If you have any questions consult your healthcare provider.

Note
The author made every attempt to be as accurate as possible in presenting this information. Below are some journal and textbook citations that may have been reviewed and used in part in the development of some of the material.

* These statements have not been evaluated by the Food and Drug Administration. This publication is not intended to diagnose, treat, cure or prevent any disease.

Citations Journal References:

Frassetto L, Morris RC Jr., Sebastian A. Diet acid load and bone health. In Nutritional Aspects of Osteoporosis, 2nd edition, Burckhardt P, Dawson-Hughes B Eds. Academic Press San Diego, CA 2004.

Frassetto L, Morris RC Jr., Sebastian A. Stone age diets for the 21st century: The effects of diet-induced, potassium-replete, chloride-sufficient, low-grade metabolic alkalosis. In Nutritional Aspects of Osteoporosis, 2nd edition, Burckhardt P, Dawson-Hughes B Eds. Academic Press San Diego, CA 2004.

Frassetto LA, Morris RC, Jr, Sebastian A. A practical approach to acid production and renal acid excretion in humans. Semin Nephrol (accepted 2004).

Frassetto L, Morris RC Jr., Sebastian A., Potassium Bicarbonate Reduces Urinary Nitrogen Excretion in Postmenopausal Women. Journal of Clinical Endocrinology and Metabolism
Vol. 82, No. 1, The Endocrine Society, 1997

Sebastian A., Morris RC Jr., Improved Mineral Balance and Skeletal Metabolism in Postmenopausal Women Treated with Potassium Bicarbonate, The New England Journal of Medicine, Vol. 330; No. 25, June 23, 1994

Frassetto L,, Sebastian A., Age and Systemic Acid-Base Equilibrium: Analysis of Published Data, Journals of Gerontology Series A: Biological Sciences and Medical Sciences, Vol 51, Issue 1 B91-B99.

Singh, Gurkirpal and Rosen Ramey, Dena. NSAID Induced Gastrointestinal Complications: The ARAMIS Perspective - 1997 . The Journal of Rheumatology, Vol. 25, Supplement 51. May 1998. (ARAMIS:Arthritis Rheumatism Aging Medical Information Service)

Lipsky PE, Brooks P, Crofford LJ et al. Unresolved issues in the role of cyclooxygenase-2 in normal physiologic processes and disease. Arch Intern Med 2000; 160: 913-20.

FitzGerald GA. COX-2 and beyond: approaches to prostaglandin inhibition in human disease. Nat Rev Drug Discov 2003; 2: 879-90)

FitzGerald GA. Coxibs and cardiovascular disease. N Engl J Med 2004; 351: 1709-11.)

Cheng Y, Austin SC, Rocca B et al. Role of prostacyclin in the cardiovascular response to t hromboxane A2. Science 2002; 296: 539-41.

Buerkle MA, Lehrer S, Sohn HY et al. Selective inhibition of cyclooxygenase-2 enhances platelet adhesion in hamster arterioles in vivo. Circulation 2004; 110: 2053-9.

Alcindor D, Krolikowski JG, Pagel PS, Warltier DC, Kersten JR. Cyclooxygenase-2 mediates ischemic, anesthetic, and pharmacologic preconditioning in vivo. Anesthesiology 2004; 100:547-54.

Textbook References:
Fuhrman, Joel L; Eat To Live, 1st Edition, Time Warner Book Group, New York, NY 10020, January 2005

Fitzgerald, Randall; The Hundred Year Lie, 1st Edition, Dutton, Published by Penguin Group New York, NY, 2006

Campbell, Colin T; The China Study, 1st Edition, BenBella Books, Dallas, Tx 75206, 2004

Robbins, John; The Food Revolution, 1st Edition, Conari Press, Berkeley, CA 94710, 2001

McDougall, John A; The McDougall Program, 15th Edition, Harper & Row, New York, NY,1985

Dr. Donald L. Hayes, D.C.
is Founder and President of Wellness Watchers International, Inc. Dr. Hayes received his Bachelor of Science Degree from the University of Oregon and Doctorate in Chiropractic from Western States Chiropractic College in 1977.

After 20 years of private practice, Dr. Hayes founded a management company that developed educational programs, products and training for healthcare providers in the field of alternative and complementary medicine.

Wellness Watchers was founded with a mission to improve health and well-being by assisting others in reaching their health potential through natural "whole food products," education and lifestyle programs.

Dr. Hayes has also created other Practice Programs so that healthcare providers and organizations can provide innovative and exciting health awareness programs to easily measure and monitor the health status of individuals.

Dr. Hayes lectures nationally and internationally to public groups, doctors and corporations on the subject of functional medicine, applied nutrition, wellness, and anti-aging strategies. His vision inspires others to aim for a better quality of life for themselves and their families.